はしがき

　「あなたは英語が好きですか」と聞かれて皆さんはどう答えますか。「好きで得意」「好きだけど苦手」「嫌いだけど得意」「嫌いで苦手」…さまざまな答えが返ってきそうです。いずれにせよ，いったん英語を学び始めたのですから，きちんとした英語力はつけたいですよね。

　ところで，その「きちんとした英語力」とは何でしょうか。それは，「正しい」英語を話したり，書いたりすることができるようになることです。そして，「正確に，素早く」英語を読んだり，聞き取れるようになることです。言い換えれば，英語を使って「教養ある」そして「実用的な」コミュニケーションを行うことができるようになること，それが「きちんとした英語力」が身についた状態と言えるのです。

　それでは，どのようにしたらその「きちんとした英語力」は身につくのでしょうか。「英文法をマスターすること」。それがこの答えです。ただし，単に英文法の知識だけを覚えていればそれでよいというわけではありません。英文法を理解し，運用し，身につける。これが大切です。そして，その際に意識しておきたいのは，その英文法を使って何ができるのかということです。これが英文法を"Can-do"の観点から捉える見方です。

　本書はこのCan-doの視点を軸にして，英語コミュニケーションに役立つ表現や文法を習得し，その能力をより効果的に伸ばすことをねらいとしています。たとえば，「人に助言や指示することができる」というCan-doをテーマにすれば，ターゲットとなる文法項目は must, should, had better などの助動詞および助動詞相当語句となり，あるいは表現としては I would advise you to .... や Why don't you ...? などになって，これらを中心に学習することになります。

　本書ではこのように，英語を使って何ができるかという機能面（Can-do）

に着目し，英語コミュニケーション能力を高めるための言語活動を展開することで，皆さんが今持っている英語力をさらに伸ばすことを意図しています。

　先に述べた英語を使って教養ある実用的なコミュニケーションを行うためには，このCan-doという英語表現の機能面を意識しながら英文法や重要表現をマスターし，習熟することが不可欠です。本書は，そのための演習や活動を豊富に提供しています。

　本書が皆さんのお役に立つことを心から願っています。

2025年1月

萩野　俊哉

本書の構成と使い方

本書は 10 単元の Can-do からなっており，それぞれの単元は，次の 5 つの柱を中心として構成されています。

① DIALOGUE

各 Can-do の見出しに関連する文法事項や表現が含まれている文章を会話形式で示しています。会話は，それらの文法や表現が，実際にどのように使われるのかを生き生きと示してくれます。会話の流れ・文脈を追いながら，その文法事項や表現がどのように使われているのかを理解し，確認しましょう。実際に口に出して登場人物になったつもりで会話を音読してみると理解がより深まり，しっかりと身につきます。ぜひ，音読してみましょう。

② 表現のまとめ

ターゲットとなる Can-do に関連する文法事項や表現について，簡単な解説と例文をあげて整理し，まとめてあります。高校生の時に習ったものばかりですので，よく思い出して，必要に応じて学習参考書などを参照しながら確認するとよいでしょう。

③ EXERCISES

ターゲットとなる Can-do に関連する文法事項や表現に習熟するための演習問題です。語句を選択して空所を埋め，英文を完成する問題や，語句の並べ替え問題，そして英作文の問題などがあります。また，Can-do に沿って英語で自由に表現する設問も用意されています。

④ **LISTENING & TALKING, WRITING**

　ターゲットとなる Can-do に関連する文法事項や表現を含む英語の文章を聞き取ったり，話したり，書いたりする活動です。TF（True or False）問題や英語での Q&A などがあります。また，聞きとった内容をもとにペアで話し合ったり，自分の経験や意見，考えなどを英語でまとめて書く活動もあります。加えて，次の PAIR & GROUP WORK につながる話し合いや，書く活動が含まれている場合もあります。

　なお，Listening については，スクリプトに沿って授業者が授業中に実際にリアルタイムで行うか，事前に録音をして行うなどしていただきたいと思います。

⑤ **PAIR & GROUP WORK**

　ターゲットとなる Can-do に関連するコミュニケーション活動です。ペアやグループで行う活動となります。準備や手順などについては先生の指示に従ってください。ワークシートを使って行う活動もあります。また，自己評価と他者への評価を行うためのシートも用意されています。有効に使って，各自のレベルアップにつなげてほしいと思います。

　なお，大学の講義では，1つの講義を45分間として，各単元を3回の講義で行うことを想定しています。各単元ごとに，DIALOGUE・表現のまとめ・EXERCISES で1講義，LISTENING & TALKING, WRITING で1講義，PAIR & GROUP WORK で1講義で，計3講義です。

　通年ではなく，たとえば半期での講義スケジュールであれば，次の①もしくは②のような対応が考えられます。あるいは，①と②を組み合わせてもよいでしょう。

　①奇数単元を講義で，偶数単元を自学自習で行う。

　②各単元においては，DIALOGUE・表現のまとめ・EXERCISES・

LISTENING & TALKING, WRITING を取捨選択して行い，PAIR & GROUP WORK については講義時間に余裕ができたときに行う。

　また，本書は大学・短大生のみならず，高校生や一般の方々向けにも使うことができると思います。対象を限定せず，広く設定していますので，自由にアレンジしながら有効に使っていただければ幸いです。

　本書には、下記１の付属資料を用意しています。どうぞご活用いただきたいと思います。本書の教師用見本として紙媒体を、また、下記２の別冊のお求めは、eigyo@kyoiku.co.jp へご連絡ください。
1　本書巻末ワークシートおよび評価シート
　　ワークシートは主に PAIR & GROUP WORK を行う際に用います。また、評価シートについては PAIR & GROUP WORK を終えた後、自己評価と他者評価の２つの観点に沿って評価を行う際に用います。具体的な使い方については、次の別冊「教師用資料」を参照してください。
2　解答・解説・教師用資料（別冊）
　　特に PAIR & GROUP WORK について、それぞれの活動のねらいおよび指導の手順や内容、そして教師による評価の方法などを詳しく解説しています。

Can-do English
― 英語コミュニケーション能力を高めるために ―

目　次

はしがき……………………………………………………………… *1*

本書の構成と使い方………………………………………………… *3*

Can-do 1　事実や考えを尋ねたり，述べることができる
　　　　　《関連文法事項：時制（現在・過去・未来・進行形・時制の一致）・疑問詞》
　　　　　……………………………………………………………… *11*

Can-do 2　自分の考えや感情も含めて，経験を述べることができる
　　　　　　　　　　　　　　　　　《関連文法事項：時制（完了形）》
　　　　　……………………………………………………………… *16*

Can-do 3　人に助言や指示することができる
　　　　　　　　　　　《関連文法事項：助動詞および助動詞相当語句》
　　　　　……………………………………………………………… *22*

Can-do 4　情報の自然な流れを意識して述べることができる
　　　　　　　　　　　　　　　　　　　　《関連文法事項：受動態》
　　　　　……………………………………………………………… *28*

Can-do 5　好きか嫌いかを尋ねたり，述べたりすることができる
　　　　　　　　　　　《関連文法事項：準動詞（不定詞・分詞・動名詞）》
　　　　　……………………………………………………………… *34*

Can-do 6　物事について比較して尋ねたり，述べたりすることができる
　　　　　　　　　　　　　　　　　　　　　《関連文法事項：比較》
　　　　　……………………………………………………………… *39*

Can-do 7 情報を追加して説明することができる

　《関連文法事項：後置修飾関係（関係詞，準動詞（分詞・不定詞），前置詞句，接続詞，つなぎの副詞》

　………………………………………………………………………… *45*

Can-do 8 現実と想像上の出来事を区別して述べることができる

　　　　　　　　　　　《関連文法事項：仮定法と直説法》

　………………………………………………………………………… *50*

Can-do 9 人の言葉を別の人に伝えることができる

　　　　　　　　　　　《関連文法事項：時制の一致と話法》

　………………………………………………………………………… *56*

Can-do 10 物事を順序だてて論理的に説明し，自分の考えや感情を表現することができる

　　　　　　　　　《関連文法事項：接続詞，形容詞，副詞》

　………………………………………………………………………… *62*

各 Can-do の評価シートとワークシート

　………………………………………………………………………… *68*

Can-do 1
事実や考えを尋ねたり，述べることができる

《関連文法事項：時制（現在・過去・未来・進行形・時制の一致）・疑問詞》

DIALOGUE　situation：at school

Steve：Hi, Ann. **I'll tell you the news.** I bet you'll find it interesting.
Ann　：Oh, **what is it?**
Steve：**I found a new live music club.**
Ann　：Really? **What's it like?**
Steve：Well, it's real small but the prices are decent.
Ann　：**How's the atmosphere?**
Steve：Great! **Actually, our favorite band, *the Space Vader*, performs there regularly.**
Ann　：Wow! Then, **I think we should go there sometime.**

日本語訳　場面：学校で

スティーブ：やあ，アン。いいニュースがあるんだ。きっと興味が引かれると思うよ。
アン　　　：えっ，何それ？
スティーブ：新しいライブハウスを見つけたのさ。
アン　　　：ホント？　どんな感じ？
スティーブ：えーっとね，ちょっと狭いんだけど，そんなに高くないところだよ。

アン　　　：雰囲気はどう？
スティーブ：最高だよ。実は，僕たちのお気に入りのバンド，「スペース・ベイダー」がそこで定期的に演奏するんだよ。
アン　　　：すてき！　じゃ，いつかそこに一緒に行かなきゃね。

表現のまとめ

①事実を尋ねたり，述べるときの表現（動詞の現在形や過去形を使う）

Oh, what *is* it? / I *found* a new live music club. / Actually, our favorite band, *the Space Vader*, *performs* there regularly.

②考え（意見・感想・意志・予定など）を尋ねたり，述べるときの表現

I *think* we should go there sometime.

※ In my opinion [view], … / From my viewpoint [point of view], …なども使える。

I'*ll* tell you the news.

※ will は「意志未来」を表し，「～するつもり」という意味。

What's it like? / *How's* the atmosphere?

※ what や how などの疑問詞を使って感想や意見を引き出す。

EXERCISES

1　空所に入る最も適切な語句を，それぞれ下から選んで，番号で答えなさい。

(1) Water (　　) at a temperature of 100 degrees centigrade.
　　① boils　② is boiling　③ was boiling　④ boiled

(2) A : What did you do last night?
　　B : I watched TV, practiced the piano, and (　　) my homework.
　　① do　② did　③ have done　④ would do

(3) A : (　　) did you like the coffee?
　　B : Very much. It was very good.

① How　② What　③ When　④ Why

2　次の日本語を英訳しなさい。
(1) 彼女は大学生のときに3回アメリカへ行った。
　　She _____ when she was a college student.
(2) 彼は一生懸命勉強しなければ，その試験に合格しないと思います。
　　If he _____ study hard, I _____ pass the exam.
(3) サリーと彼女の友人はスペインへ行く予定です。
　　Sally and her friend _____ Spain.
(4) 私たちはシェイクスピアは1564年に生まれたと学校で学んだ。
　　We learned at school that Shakespeare _____ .

3　次の会話文の空所に入る最も適切な語句を，下から選んで番号で答えなさい。

A：You look depressed. What happened?
B：My smartphone was taken away by Mr. Suzuki.
A：Oh, why?
B：Because I was using it during his lesson.
A：So you cannot complain about it. It's against the school regulation.
B：I know. But (　　　) of this kind of matter? I mean, do you really think we need to be banned from using a smartphone at school?

　① Do you say any ideas　　② How do you think
　③ What do you speak　　　④ What's your opinion

《Plus One Activity》
上の会話のBの最後のセリフに続くAのセリフを考えて英語で書きなさい。

_____
_____
_____

LISTENING & TALKING

(1) You are wondering if you will stay at this hotel, and you want to find out about it. Write down some questions as below.
- Is there a swimming pool in the hotel?
- Is the Wi-Fi service available in the hotel?
- Does the hotel allow pets to stay with us? etc.

(2) You will listen to three people talking about the hotel.
Question 1 Which of your questions written above do they answer?
Question 2 Is this a good hotel for
— a group of students?
— someone on a business trip?
— a retired couple?

(3) Do you want to stay at the hotel? Why or why not? Form pairs and exchange opinions with your partner.

GROUP WORK

Step 1

Write as many sentences as possible describing your future plans. Refer to the examples.

(Examples)

① I will work in a café after graduating from college.

② I'm going to go to the U.S. this summer vacation.

③ I think I should stay home and study hard this weekend.

If possible, add a *because* clause to your sentence in order to show a reason like this:

①' I will work in a café after graduating from college, because my parents run it and ask me to help them.

②' I'm going to go to the U.S. this summer vacation, because my cousin is in New York and he invited me to visit him.

③' I think I should stay home and study hard this weekend, because our class has an English test next Monday.

Step 2

(1) Make a group of three or four people. In your group, introduce to the other members the sentences you wrote in Step 1 above, and from those sentences choose five sentences all the members of your group are impressed with or strongly interested in.

(2) Have one of your group members introduce the group's five sentences to the whole class. Talk as a class about any sentences that are especially interesting or surprising.

Can-do 2
自分の考えや感情も含めて，経験を述べることができる

《関連文法事項：時制（完了形）》

DIALOGUE　situation : at school

Jiro : Hi, Jim. Anne said that you like to play soccer.
Jim : Yes, I like the game very much. In fact, I played for two years on my high school team.
Jiro : Did you? **I haven't played** very much, but I really enjoy the game.
Jim : It's a very fine game! It has been popular in Europe for a long time.
Jiro : It is also very popular in South America, isn't it?
Jim : Yes, and the South American teams are very strong.

日本語訳　場面：学校で

ジロー：やあ，ジム。アンが言っていたけど，君サッカーをするのが好きなんだね。
ジム　：うん。大好きだよ。実は，高校のとき2年間やっていたんだ。
ジロー：ふーん，そうなの。僕はあまりやったことはないけど，サッカーは本当に楽しいよね。
ジム　：本当にすばらしいスポーツだよ。ヨーロッパではずっと長い間人気を保ち続けているよ。
ジロー：南米でもずいぶん人気があるよね。

ジム　：そうだね。南米のチームはとても強いよ。

表現のまとめ　経験を述べるときの表現。

①I *haven't played* (soccer) very much.
　（私はあまりサッカーをやったことはありません。）
　【解説】現在完了形（have / has + 過去分詞）で現在までの経験を表す。
②I recognized him easily, because I *had met* him before.
　（私は彼とは以前会ったことがあったので，簡単に彼を見分けられた）
　【解説】過去完了形（had + 過去分詞）で，過去のあるときまでの経験を表す。
③If I watch this movie on TV, I *will have watched* it three times.
　（もしこの映画をテレビで見れば，3回見たことになるでしょう。）
　【解説】未来完了形（will have + 過去分詞）で，未来のあるときまでの経験を表す。
④その他の表現
　He *experienced* big success when he was young.
　※ experience は動詞。
　=He had *experience* of big success when he was young.
　※ experience は名詞。
　（彼は若いときに大成功を経験した。）

EXERCISES

1　空所に入る最も適切な語句を，それぞれ下から選んで，番号で答えなさい。

(1) If I go to Europe again, I (　　) there four times.
　　① go　② went　③ have been　④ will have been
(2) That was the finest view (　　).
　　① I never saw　② I had ever seen
　　③ I have never seen　④ I will ever see

(3) Have you (　　) your way in a strange town?
　　① losing　② had lost　③ have lost　④ ever lost

2　各文の（　　）内の語句を正しく並べ替えなさい。
(1) 奈良にちょうど行ってきたところですが，これから京都へ行きます。
　　※1語不要
　　We (to / have / been / gone / Nara) and now we are leaving for Kyoto.
　　_____

(2) 初めて米国に来たのはいつだったか教えてください。※2語不要
　　Tell me (came / come / have / to / when / you) the United States for the first time.
　　_____

3　次の日本語を英訳しなさい。
(1) このパソコンを買ってそろそろ1年になるけど，まだ使ったことがないんだ。
　　It's nearly a year since I _____ this personal computer but I _____ yet.
(2) A：富士山に登ったことはありますか。
　　　_____ Mt. Fuji?
　　B：ええ。18歳の誕生日に登ったことがあります。
　　　Yes, _____. I _____ on my eighteenth birthday.

4　会話が成立するように，5～10語の文を書きなさい。
　　A：What have you never done before?
　　B：_____
　　　_____

LISTENING & WRITING

1. Keiko and a cabin attendant are talking in the airplane before departure. Listen carefully and share the information you have caught with your partner.

   2人の会話の内容と合う英文には（　　）内にT（True）を記入して全文を書き写し，合わないものについてはF（False）を記入して正しく書き換え，はっきりしないものには？（Question Mark）を記入して疑問文に書き換えなさい。

   1. Keiko wore her seat belt before she is talked to by the cabin attendant. （　　）
   _____

   2. Keiko is calm and relaxed because she has been to a foreign country before. （　　）
   _____

   3. The cabin attendant is surprised to find that Keiko has been learning English for three years but cannot speak English well. （　　）
   _____

   4. Keiko has got confident in her English thanks to the cabin attendant. （　　）
   _____

2. 以下の（例）のように，ワークシートの1.にある4つの英文の下線部を，それぞれ自由に埋めなさい。ワークシートには氏名を書かないこと。

（例）1. I have been to Hokkaido before.
　　　2. I have seen a shooting star before.

3. I have read *Hino-tori* by Osamu Tezuka before.

4. I have heard about my parents' marriage before.

1. …「今まで行ったことがあるところで印象に残っている場所」

2. …「今までに見たことのあるものの中で印象に残っているもの（例：映画やテレビなどを含む）」

3. …「今まで読んだことのある本やその他のものの中で印象に残っているもの」

4. …「今まで聞いたことのあるものの中で印象に残っているもの（例：ニュースや音楽などを含む）」

PAIR & GROUP WORK

ワークシートを使って進めなさい。

1. 次の（例）にならって会話をして，ワークシートの1. の4つの英文を書いた人物を特定しなさい。なお，ワークシートは会話をする相手に見せてはいけません。

（例）A：Have you been to Hokkaido before?
　　　B：Yes, I have.
　　　A：Have you seen a shooting star before?
　　　B：No, I haven't.
　　　A：OK. Thank you.
　　　B：You're welcome.（そして，Aは別の人とまた最初の1.から質問をしていく）

2. 上の1. で特定された人にインタビューをします。次の（例）にならって，そのときの感想（考えや感情）を引き出して，メモしましょう。

（例）A：When did you go to Hokkaido?
　　　B：I went there three years ago.

Can-do 2　自分の考えや感情も含めて，経験を述べることができる　*21*

　　A : How did you feel about Hokkaido?
　　B : It was so huge! I was very surprised. And I thought people there were all kind.
　　A : Oh, why did you think so?
　　　　…

～相手の考えや感情を引き出すときの質問例～
・How did you feel about ～ ?
・How did you feel when S + V ...?
・What did you think about [of] ～ (when S + V ...)?
・Were you happy / angry / sad / surprised ...etc. at that time?
・Were you happy / angry / sad / surprised ...etc. when S + V ...?

3. 上の2. でとったメモを参考に，グループ内や全体の前でインタビューの結果を発表しましょう。その後，まとめとしてインタビューの結果を50～70語程度の英語でワークシートの3. に書きましょう。

（例）I had an interview with Keiko. She has been to Hokkaido. She went there three years ago. She was very surprised to find that Hokkaido was so huge. She thought that people there were all kind because …

Can-do 3
人に助言や指示することができる

《関連文法事項：助動詞および助動詞相当語句》

DIALOGUE　situation：on the street in New York City

Alice： Hi! I haven't seen you around here before.
Mari： Well, I just got in this week. I'm Mari Sato.
Alice： Glad to meet you. I'm Alice Baker. Where are you from?
Mari： I come from Japan. Are you from New York?
Alice： Yes and no. My home is in upstate New York, not the city. It's right near Niagara Falls.
Mari： Really? I want to visit Niagara Falls sometime in the future.
Alice： Good idea. **You ought to visit it if you have a chance.** It's so fantastic!

日本語訳　場面：道端で

アリス：こんにちは。このあたりではお見かけしたことないわね。
マリ　：ええ，今週やって来たばかりなんです。佐藤マリといいます。
アリス：はじめまして。私はアリス・ベーカー。どこのご出身？
マリ　：日本です。あなたはニューヨークのご出身？
アリス：どちらとも言えないわね。実家はニューヨーク市ではなくて，ニューヨーク州の北部なの。ナイアガラの滝のすぐ近くなのよ。
マリ　：本当ですか？　私，将来いつかナイアガラの滝を見に行きたいと

思っているんです。

アリス：それはいい考えね。機会があれば訪れてみるといいわ。とっても素晴らしいわよ！

表現のまとめ

人に助言や指示するときの表現。

You *ought to* visit it if you have a chance.

cf. You *should / must / need to* visit it if you have a chance.

You *had better* visit it if you have a chance.

You *might as well* visit it if you have a chance.

It might be an idea to visit it if you have a chance.

It is [would be] better / necessary to visit it if you have a chance.

I would advise you to visit it if you have a chance.

Why don't you visit it if you have a chance.

EXERCISES

1　空所に入る最も適切な語句を、それぞれ下から選んで、番号で答えなさい。

(1) You (　　　) go even if you don't want to.

　① can　② must　③ cannot　④ must not

(2) You (　　　) leave your heavy clothing here as it is warmer there.

　① don't have to　② has to　③ won't　④ should

(3) You (　　　) talk too much.

　① had not better　② had better not

　③ had better not to　④ had not better to

(4) It takes so long by train. You (　　　) as well fly.

　① should　② might　③ can　④ would

(5) You (　　) to be noisy at this time of the night.
　　① do not ought　② ought not　③ should not　④ not ought

2　次の日本語を英訳しなさい。
(1) 君は出かける前に仕事を片づけてしまうべきだ。
　　You _____ before going out.
(2) 彼はその会合に出席すべきでした。
　　He _____ attended the meeting.
(3) 外見だけで人を判断してはいけない。
　　You _____ only because of their appearances.
(4) A : Tom is sick in bed and feels very nervous about his health.
　　B : 彼には本当のことを言わない方がいいと思いますよ。
　　_____

3　会話が成立するように，5～10語の文を書きなさい。
　　A : I'm feverish and have a sore throat.
　　B : _____
　　_____

LISTENING & WRITING

　John and Mary are an old married couple, who have never got out of their state in the US. They are now talking about the trip with each other at home in the U.S. Listen to them carefully, and follow the directions below :

1　Based on the content of the dialogue, decide whether each following sentence is true (T) or false (F).
(1) John and Mary have already learned a lot about Japan and

Japanese culture. It is certain that they will enjoy themselves in Japan.

(　　)

(2) John and Mary don't believe that Japanese people use knives and forks.

(　　)

(3) Mary believes that *Maikos*, who are well-known in Kyoto, are everywhere in Tokyo and that it will be easy to take pictures with them.

(　　)

(4) John doesn't expect that he will be able to meet *ninjas* and talk with them easily even in Japan.

(　　)

(5) John and Mary will reserve the restaurants they are going to go to in Japan.

(　　)

2　The U.S. is a big country, and you may meet people like John and Mary. Please give them some advice so that they will be able to have a nicer and more comfortable trip to Japan.

_____
_____
_____

PAIR & GROUP WORK

Imagine that you're in the U.S. and talking to an American who is going to visit Japan for the first time.

- ▶ Think of questions the American might ask.
- ▶ Take turns giving advice about the habits the American would have to get used to.

For example, talk about some of these things :

◆ *Getting into Japan* :
  passport,
  customs,
  visa,
  vaccinations

◆ *Transportation* :
  public transportation,
  driving a car,
  taking taxis,
  cycling

◆ *Shopping* :
  commodity prices,
  kinds of stores,
  finding bargains,
  paying with cash, a credit card or electronic money

◆ *Eating* :
  restaurants,
  cafes,
  table manners,
  meal times

◆ *Social behavior* :
  meeting people [strangers],
  visiting people at home,
  inviting people out

◆ *Language* :
  where English can be used,
  where the Japanese language should be used

◆ *Gestures* :
  different meanings of gestures in Japan and other countries

Example

A (an American) : Do I always have to pay with cash in shopping in Japan?

B (you) : Well, in some stores you don't have to. You can pay with a credit card or electronic money there. But in the other ones, you have to. I think you should ask a clerk before paying.

A (an American) : Oh, I see. Thank you so much.

Can-do 4
情報の自然な流れを意識して述べることができる

《関連文法事項：受動態》

DIALOGUE　situation：at a restaurant

A: What should we order? Do you feel like a hamburger?
B: That sounds good. But just between us, I'm worried about gaining weight.
A: Really? But you're not fat! What's more, you worry too much about your body. **You are influenced too much by beauty magazines.**
B: Well then, instead of a hamburger, I'll have turkey sandwiches.

日本語訳　場面：レストランで

A：何にする？　君はハンバーガーかな？
B：いいわね。でも，ここだけの話，太るのが心配なの。
A：ほんとう？　でも，君は太ってなんかいないよ。それにまあ言わせてもらえば，君って自分の身体のことちょっと気にしすぎじゃないかなあ。女性雑誌に影響されすぎなんじゃない？
B：う～ん，それじゃ，ハンバーガーじゃなくて，ターキーのサンドイッチにするわ。

表現のまとめ

　原則として英文の自然な情報の流れは，旧情報から始めてその後に新情報が続く。上記の You are influenced too much by beauty magazines. の You は前文および前々文の you と同じ You である。つまり，旧情報から文を始め，その後に新しい情報をつなげている。これは情報の流れの原則に合致しており，その流れを作るために重要な役割をしているのが受動態という文構造である。

（類例）

(1) The school looks very old. When *was* it *built* ?
　（この学校はとても古そうですね。いつ建てられたんですか？）

(2) Ms. White is very popular in school. She *is liked* by everybody.
　（ホワイトさんは学校でとても人気者で，彼女はみんなに好かれている。）

(3) A : What happens to the cars made in this factory?
　（この工場で作られた車はどうなるんですか？）
　B : Most of them *are sent* abroad.
　（ほとんどが海外に送られるんですよ。）

(4) A : Oh, how beautiful these flowers are! And I like the vase, too. It *is made* of glass, isn't it?
　（わあ，なんてきれいな花！ それにこの花びんも気に入ったな。ガラスで作られているんだよね？）
　B : Sorry, but it *is made* of plastic, not glass.
　（いや，これはガラスじゃなくてプラスチックだよ。）

EXERCISES

1　各文の（　　　）内の語句を正しく並べ替えなさい。

(1) ヒロシは今日もまた学校に遅刻して，佐藤先生からもう二度と遅刻しないように注意されました。

Hiroshi was late for school today again. He (be / late / not / to / told / was) again by Mr. Sato.

(2) 彼は内緒で逃げ出そうとしたが，家から出るところを見られた。
Though he had tried to run away secretly, he (coming / of / out / seen / the house / was).

(3) ブラウン氏には3人の娘がいて，そのうちの1人は有名な歌手と結婚している。
※1語不要
Mr. Brown has three daughters. One of (a / them / married / marries / to / is) famous singer.

2 次の日本語を英訳しなさい。
(1) 「彼はなぜ怒っているの？」「長いこと待たされたからさ。」
"Why is he angry?" "Because he ＿＿＿＿＿＿＿＿＿＿ for a long time."
(2) 彼は年老いて健康を害している。息子さんからの世話が必要だ。
He is old and unhealthy. He has to ＿＿＿＿＿＿＿＿＿＿ by his son.
(3) やっと著書を書き上げた。多くの人から読んでもらえる本になればと願っている。
Finally, I've written the book. I hope it ＿＿＿＿＿＿＿＿＿＿ by many people.
(4) A : I asked the way to the station, but nobody answered me properly.
B : 多くの日本人は外国人から英語で話しかけられると緊張してしまう

んです。
Many Japanese people get nervous when ＿＿＿＿＿＿ in English.

(5) A : This temple is beautiful. How old is it?
B : 1343年建立です。
＿＿＿＿＿＿＿＿＿＿＿＿＿＿＿＿＿＿＿＿＿＿＿＿＿．

3 会話が成立するように，5〜10語の文を書きなさい。
A : Ms Sato, our teacher, is always kind and thoughtful.
B : That's why ＿＿＿＿＿＿＿＿＿＿＿＿＿＿＿＿＿ by everybody.

LISTENING & WRITING

Keiko is staying at Jane's house with her family in the U.S. They are now talking at Jane's home party. Listen to them and answer the following questions.

1 会話の内容と合うように空所を補い，英文を完成させなさい。なお，(   )内で与えられた語句を適切な形に変えて使いなさい。

(1) The pieces of paper ＿＿＿＿＿＿(fold) by Keiko to make ＿＿＿＿＿＿, dolls, boats and so on.
(2) Scissors or paste ＿＿＿＿＿＿＿＿＿ (use) to do *origami*.
(3) The paper crane ＿＿＿＿＿＿＿＿＿ (make) by Keiko ＿＿＿＿＿＿＿＿ (praise) by Jane.
(4) Keiko explained to Jane that *origami* ＿＿＿＿＿＿ (often call) "paper art."

2 会話の内容と合うように下から適語を選び，必要ならば適切な形に変えて空所を補い，英文を完成させなさい。

(1) Jane said Keiko _____ at the news she was going to say.

(2) The news is that Jane and her family _____ the Grand Canyon next weekend and Keiko _____ to join them.

(3) The Grand Canyon _____ to many Japanese tourists to the U.S.

(4) The Grand Canyon _____ to _____ with Japanese people.

> crowd, invite, know, say, surprise, visit

【注】the Grand Canyon：グランドキャニオン（米国 Arizona（アリゾナ）州北西部のコロラド川流域の大峡谷）

PAIR & GROUP WORK

ワークシートを使って進めなさい。

1. ペアになってA，Bを決めなさい。Aの人はワークシート(1)が，Bの人はワークシート(2)が配られます。配られてもお互いにワークシートを見せ合ってはいけません。

2. ワークシートには4人の人物の表情が描かれています。これからペアでなぜそれぞれがそのような表情になったのかを説明し合います。次のページに例を示します。

Can-do 4　情報の自然な流れを意識して述べることができる　33

ワークシート (1)

Jane : sad

She was scolded by her mother.
_____

ワークシート (2)

Jane : sad

[her mother / scold]
*scold 〜：〜を叱る

(例)
(下線部のあるシートを持つ人から会話を始める。この例ではワークシート (1) を持つ A の人から始める)

Student A : What happened to Jane? She looks sad.
Student B : She was scolded by her mother.

・下線部のあるシートを持つ人（上の（例）では A）は，"What happened to 〜? He/She looks 〜."と質問し，相手の答えを聞き取って下線部を埋める。

・イラストの下に [　/　] 内で語句が示されているシートを持つ人（上の（例）ではワークシート (2) を持つ B）は，それらの語句を使って相手の質問に答える。

3. ペアで4人の人物のうちの1人を取り上げ，上の2. の会話をさらに広げて50〜80語程度の創作 skit を作ります。

4. 4つのペアからなるグループを作り，それぞれのグループ内で上の3. で創作した skit をペアごとに発表し合います。その後，各グループの代表ペアが，クラス全体の前で発表します。

Can-do 5
好きか嫌いかを尋ねたり，述べたりすることができる

《関連文法事項：準動詞（不定詞・分詞・動名詞）》

DIALOGUE　situation：on the way home

A：How did you like the movie we saw at school today?
B：I thought it was good. **I normally don't like seeing historical movies,** but I found this one to be quite interesting. How did you like it?
A：**I hate admitting it,** but I missed most of it.
B：What do you mean?
A：**I like watching movies,** but somehow today I fell asleep ten minutes into the movie and didn't wake up until it was almost finished.
B：Really? I didn't notice that you were sleeping.
A：Yeah, I just hope we don't have a test on it.

日本語訳　場面：家への帰り道で
A：今日，学校で見た映画，どうだった？
B：いいと思ったよ。僕はふつう歴史映画を見るのは好きじゃないんだけれど，これはなかなか面白いと思ったよ。君はどう思った？
A：認めたくないんだけど，実はほとんど見ていなかったんだよ。
B：どういうこと？

A：僕は映画を見るのは好きだけど，どういうわけか今日は映画が始まって10分したら眠っちゃって，ほとんど終わるころまで目が覚めなかったんだ。
B：本当？ 君が眠っているなんて気がつかなかったよ。
A：うん。映画についてのテストがないことを願っているよ。

表現のまとめ

好きか嫌いかを尋ねたり，述べたりするときの表現。

Do you *like* watching [to watch] movies?
— I *like* watching [to watch] movies.

　①「好き」を表現する：

　　・I *love* [*enjoy* / *adore*] watching movies.

　　・I *am keen on* watching movies.

　　・I *am fond of* watching movies.

　　・I *am crazy* [*mad* / *nuts* / *wild*] *about* watching movies.【口語的な表現】

　②「嫌い」を表現する：

　　・I *dislike* [*hate*] watching movies.

　　・I *can't stand* [*bear* / *put up with*] watching movies.

EXERCISES

1　空所に入る最も適切な語句を，それぞれ下から選んで，番号で答えなさい。

(1) The nurse (　　) enter the room because the patient was in critical condition.

　　① told us not to　　② told to us not to

　　③ said to us not to　　④ talked us not to

(2) A (　　) stone gathers no moss.

① roll　② rolled　③ roll in　④ rolling

(3) I do not like (　　) those things by him in such a rude manner.

① being told　② having told　③ telling　④ to tell

(4) Doesn't Betty's mother complain about (　　) every night?

① for your calling her up　　② that you call her up

③ you call her up　　　　　　④ your calling her up

2　各文の (　　) 内の語句を正しく並べ替えなさい。

(1) あなたが元気で暮らしていることを知ってとてもうれしいです。

I am very glad (are / getting / know / that / to / you) along well.

_____

(2) かわいがっていた子猫に死なれて彼女は一晩中泣いていた。

She (all / crying / kept / long / night) because the kitten she loved died.

_____

(3) 私たちは，電車で東京に行くことになりました。天気がこんなに悪いときに，飛行機に乗る気はしませんからね。※それぞれ1語不要。

We (a train / decided / taking / to take) to Tokyo. We (by / don't / feel / like / plane / to travel / traveling) in such bad weather.

_____

_____

3　次の条件に合うように，英語で自由に書きなさい。

　Imagine that you are a music journalist and are going to interview a famous pianist. You'll ask him some questions about his likes and dislikes. Make some of those questions as a following example：

(例) Do you like playing solo or in an orchestra?

Can-do 5 好きか嫌いかを尋ねたり，述べたりすることができる   37

LISTENING & WRITING

1 Look at the map of Egypt below. Working in groups, talk about what you know about Egypt.

(*Example*) You can see pyramids in many places in Egypt. The largest one is in Giza, which is near Cairo, the capital city of Egypt. Its name is "the Pyramid of Khufu."

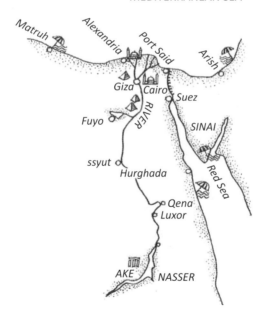

2 Hiroshi is talking with a guide in an information center in Cairo. Which places does he decide to visit? Choose the answers

from below.

a. Giza   b. Luxor   c. Qena   d. Suez   e. Port Said

3 You will listen to four sentences. Which places is the guide talking about?

① (   )   ② (   )
③ (   )   ④ (   )

4 Choose a town or a city you know fairly well. Make a list of a few interesting places to visit there. Write why they would be interesting to visit. If possible, draw a map to show where the places are. Use the worksheet 【Sheet A】.

PAIR & GROUP WORK

(1) Form pairs with another student and tell your partner about the places on the list you made in Task 4 above.

(2) After listening to your partner, choose the one place you would like to visit most of all the places on your partner's list and tell your partner why you would like to go there. Besides, choose the one place you would not like to visit and tell your partner why you would not like to go there. Take notes in the space of the worksheet 【Sheet A】.

(3) A few pairs will make their presentations of the task (2) above. The rest of the students will evaluate the performances of those pairs.

Can-do 6
物事について比較して尋ねたり，述べたりすることができる

《関連文法事項：比較》

DIALOGUE　situation：at a bus ticket counter

A：Good morning. I'd like a ticket to Chicago.
B：Okay. That'll be twenty-two dollars.
A：Twenty-two? That is **more than** I expected.
B：I know. The fare went up this month.
A：Oh, my! Everything goes up these days!

日本語訳　場面：バスの切符売り場で

A：おはようございます。シカゴ行きの切符をください。
B：はい。22 ドルになります。
A：22 ドルですって？　思ったより高いのね。
B：そうなんです。実は運賃が今月から上がりまして...
A：おやまあ！　近頃は何でも値上がりなのね！

表現のまとめ

物事について比較して尋ねたり，述べたりするときの表現。

That is *more than* I expected.

(1) John has *as many* CDs *as* I (do).
　　（ジョンは私と同じ数の CD を持っている。）（原級）

(2) That car is *less expensive than* this one.
    (あの車はこの車より高くない［安い］。)（比較級）
    = That car is not as［so］expensive as this one.
(3) She is *the fastest* runner *in* her class/ *of* all the students.
    (彼女はクラスの学生の中で／すべての学生の中で一番足が速い。)（最上級）
    = She can run *(the) fastest in* her class/ *of* all the students.（the が最上級の前に付くのは《米》）
(4) Tom has about *three times as* many CDs as I（do）.
    (トムは私の約3倍の数のCDを持っている。)〔倍数表現〕
    = Tom has about *three times more* CDs *than* I（do）.
(5) *The longer* you stay in London, *the more attractive* it becomes to you.
    (ロンドンは長くいればいるほど, 魅力的な街であることがわかってくる。)
(6) He is *more wise than clever.*（= He is wise *rather than* clever.）
    (彼は頭の回転が速い（clever）というより思慮深い（wise）。)
(7) A whale is *no more* a fish *than* a horse is（a fish）.
    (馬が魚でないのと同じように, 鯨も魚ではない。) ※いわゆる「鯨構文」である。
    = A whale is *not* a fish *any more than* a horse is（a fish）.
(8) This lake is *deepest* at this point.
    (この湖はここのポイントが一番深い。)
    ((比較)) This lake is *the* deepest in the world.
    (この湖は世界で一番深い。)
(9) She is *a most popular* idol in Japan.
    (彼女は日本でとても有名なアイドルだ。) ※ most = very

Can-do 6 物事について比較して尋ねたり，述べたりすることができる 41

EXERCISES

1 空所に入る最も適切な語句を，それぞれ下から選んで，番号で答えなさい。

(1) Tom has collected (　　　) stamps as I have.
   ① twice as many　② twice so many
   ③ as many twice　④ as much twice

(2) (　　　) went on, the more tired the players became.
   ① The long game　② The longer game
   ③ The longer the game　④ The longest the game

2 各文の (　　　) 内の語句を正しく並べ替えなさい。

(1) 若いときに受けた印象ほど，いつまでも鮮やかに心に残るものはない。
   Nothing remains (more / in our minds / than / the impressions / vividly / we received) when we were young.
   _____

(2) この冬は10年ぶりの寒さだそうです。
   I hear (coldest / is / the / this / winter) we have had in the past ten years.
   _____

3 次の日本語を英訳しなさい。

(1) ここにいても家にいるのと同じで，危険なことなんてありませんよ。
   You are _____ in danger here _____ at home.

(2) ジェフとジェニーは，ハワイの叔父さんを訪れるためにできるだけたくさんのお金を貯めた。
   Jeff and Jenny saved _____ they could to visit their uncle in Hawaii.

4 会話が成立するように，5〜10語の文を書きなさい。
A : I'm going to take an important test tomorrow. So, I'm nervous now.
B : Just take it easy. The more nervous you are, _____
_____.

LISTENING & WRITING

1 Keiko, who finished studying at high school in the U.S., has come back to her school in Kyoto. She is talking with an ALT of the school, Jason, who is from England.
会話の内容と合うように，必要な語を2語補って，（　　）内の語句を並べ替えなさい。

(1) Jason thinks that Kyoto is (city / in / Japan / the).
_____

(2) In Jason's opinion, when autumn comes, ① (beautiful / becomes / Kyoto) his hometown, Edinburgh. It means that ② (beautiful / is / Kyoto) in that season.
①_____
②_____

(3) The population of Glasgow is (of / than) Edinburgh.
_____

2 Keiko, Jason and Kate, the new exchange student from London, are walking along a street toward the restaurant where they will eat dinner.
次の英文は会話の内容をまとめたものですが，それぞれ1か所誤りを含んでいます。正しい文に書き替えなさい。

Can-do 6　物事について比較して尋ねたり，述べたりすることができる

(1) No other city in Britain is so small as London.

　_____

(2) As much as seven million people live in Britain.

　_____

(3) Keiko thinks that London is beautiful rather than attractive.

　_____

(4) Kate says as people stay longer in London, it becomes less attractive to them.

　_____

PAIR & GROUP WORK

先生の指示に従い，ワークシートを使って進めなさい。

1. これから「第1回雑学クイズ王コンテスト」を行います。先生がこれからいくつか英文を読み上げます。それぞれの文の内容が正しいと思えば教科書の表表紙を，誤っていると思えば裏表紙を先生に向けて示してください。1文につき，正解すれば2点を獲得することとします。

2. 上の1. にならって，「比較」の表現を含む，クイズになる英文をペアで考えてひとつ以上作り，ワークシートの該当箇所に記入しなさい。地理や歴史や社会に関するクイズでもよいですし，次のような，たとえばクラスの友人や知り合いなどを取り上げて英文を作っても可とします。
（例）Hiroshi has four times *as many* comic books *as* I have.

3. 上の2. でペアで作成した英文をひとつ選んで，それを代表者が教室の前に出て全員に対して口頭で発表し，1. と同じ要領で「第2回雑学クイズ王コンテスト」を行います。

4. 【振り返り英作文】上の3. での他のペアの発表を聞いて，最も興味の引かれたものをひとつ取り上げて，なぜそれがおもしろいと思ったのかを100語程度でワークシートに自由に英語で書きなさい。なお，その際，その英文を発表した人の名前と彼（彼女）が実際に発表した英文を，以下の例のように必ず最初に触れるようにしなさい。

(例) I was most interested in Satoko's statement. She said, "Recently no other country in the world has been attracting more tourists than France." At first, I thought it was false, because I believed that the U.S. attracted the most tourists in the world. However, the statement turned out to be true! I like traveling, and maybe I'll visit France in the future. So, do I have to learn French as well as English? Well, it may be too tough for me!

Can-do 7
情報を追加して説明することができる

《関連文法事項：後置修飾関係（関係詞，準動詞（分詞・不定詞），前置詞句，接続詞，つなぎの副詞》

DIALOGUE　situation：the party in John's home

John	: Hello, Nobuo. Come on in. What would you like to drink?
Nobuo	: Well, I would love to have a lemonade and soda.
John	: Sure thing! I'm glad you don't stand on ceremony or have — what's the word for it in Japanese?
Nobuo	: 'Enryo'?
John	: Yes, that's it. In America, we appreciate people **who** say **what** they mean and mean **what** they say.

日本語訳　場面：ジョンの家のパーティーで

ジョン：やあ，ノブオ。さあ，入って。飲み物は何にする？
ノブオ：そうだなあ，レモネードの炭酸割りでもいただくよ。
ジョン：いいとも。君が形式ばったりせずに，つまりその，何だったっけ，日本語で。
ノブオ：「遠慮」かい？
ジョン：そうそう。その「遠慮」をしないでいてくれてうれしいよ。アメリカでは，言いたいことを，それも本音で言う人が評価されるんだ。

表現のまとめ

情報を追加して説明する。

In America, we appreciate people **who** say **what** they mean and mean **what** they say.

(1) 名詞に情報を追加して説明する。

① She ate all the cookies *in the box*.
（彼女は箱の中のクッキーを全部食べてしまった。）【前置詞句（前置詞＋名詞）】

② He is not a man *to tell you a lie*.
（彼は嘘をつくような人ではない。）【不定詞の形容詞的用法】

③ Do you know that girl *waving her hand*?
（手を振っているあの女の子を知っていますか？）【現在分詞】

④ He has a watch *made in Switzerland*.
（彼はスイス製の時計を持っている。）【過去分詞】

⑤ She has a son *who is a famous pianist*.
（彼女には有名なピアニストの息子がいる。）【関係代名詞節】

⑥ The office *where my father works* is near Tokyo Station.
（私の父が働いている会社は東京駅の近くにある。）【関係副詞節】

(2) 動詞や形容詞や副詞や文〔節〕に情報を追加して説明する。

① He lives **on Koza Gate Street in Okinawa City**.
（彼は沖縄市のコザゲート通りに住んでいる。）【前置詞句（前置詞＋名詞）】

② The festival will be put off **if it rains**.
（祭りは雨なら延期される。）【接続詞を用いた副詞節】

EXERCISES

1. 空所に入る最も適切な語句を，それぞれ下から選んで，番号で答えなさい。
(1) The girl (　　) white is a nurse.
　① in　② of　③ on　④ with
(2) There are several ways (　　) speed.
　① measure　② to measure　③ measuring　④ for measure
(3) The language (　　) in this area is difficult to understand.
　① speak　② speaking　③ spoken　④ to speak
(4) The book, (　　) I read last night, was impressive.
　① if　② that　③ what　④ which

2. 各文の (　　) 内の語句を正しく並べ替えなさい。
(1) メモをとるための鉛筆を持ってきてください。
　Please bring a pencil (a / note / to / with / write).
　_____

(2) 私は銀行がある通りの角に車をとめた。
　I parked my car (at / is / the bank / the corner / where).
　_____

(3) 宇宙旅行を楽しめるときも，じきに来るでしょう。
　Soon the time will come (can / enjoy / space / travel / we / when).
　_____

3. 次の日本語を英訳しなさい。
(1) 彼女は私のことを理解してくれる人です。
　She is _____.
(2) 通りを横切っているあの男性は私の隣人です。

The man _____ is my neighbor.

4 次の指示に従って，英語で自由に書きなさい。

You are going to introduce a friend of yours to your classmates. Write a sentence, using the following sentence pattern, and more, if possible.

"I have a friend who _____."

（例）I have a friend who *keeps a big dog as a pet in his house.*

_____

_____

LISTENING & WRITING

1 Keiko is talked to by a stranger on the street.

会話の内容と合うように，空所に適語を入れなさい。

(1) The stranger wants to (   ) to the Falcon Hotel, (   ) has opened just recently on Apple Street.

(2) The stranger is suggesting that he is one of the (   ) people (   ) like to stay at the Falcon Hotel.

(3) Keiko told the stranger to take the bus (   ) stops at the (   ) (   ).

(4) Keiko said to the stranger, "You can take (   ) bus (   ) you like as long as it stops at the post office."

2 恵子が自分の家族の写真を Jane に見せています。（   ）内の語句のうちひとつを適当な形に変えて，正しく並べ替えなさい。そして，最後の下線部（カ）に文脈を捉えて適切な英文を書きなさい。

Keiko : Here you are. This is ア（a picture / by / take / me）.
Jane　: Thanks. … Where are your parents? Is イ（the woman / a sweater / knit）your mother?
Keiko : No, she is my aunt. ウ（everyone / for / make / tea / the woman）is my mother.
Jane　: I see. Oh, you have two brothers?
Keiko : No, no. エ（a newspaper / read / the man）is my father, and オ（a snack / eat / the man）is my brother.
Jane　: Really? カ_____.

ア（　　　　　　　　　　　　　　　）
イ（　　　　　　　　　　　　　　　）
ウ（　　　　　　　　　　　　　　　）
エ（　　　　　　　　　　　　　　　）
オ（　　　　　　　　　　　　　　　）

カ_____

GROUP WORK

　チームワーク作文を行います。先生の指示に従い，ワークシートを使って進めなさい。

Can-do 8
現実と想像上の出来事を区別して述べることができる

《関連文法事項：仮定法と直説法》

DIALOGUE

① A：What are you doing?
　B：I'm filling in this application form for a Voluntary Service job. I don't know whether to type it or not using a computer.
　A：**I would. It will look much better if you type it.**
② A：It's been many years since I saw you last.
　B：I didn't recognize you at first.
　A：**I wouldn't have, either, if someone had not mentioned your name.**

日本語訳

① A：何をしているんだい？
　B：ボランティア活動の仕事の申込用紙に記入しているところさ。ワープロを使って書こうかどうしようか迷っているところなんだ。
　A：僕だったらワープロを使うな。その方がずっと見栄えがいいからね。
② A：本当に久しぶりですね。
　B：最初は君だということがわからなかったよ。
　A：もしもだれかが君の名前を口にしなかったら，僕も気づかないところだった。

表現のまとめ

1. 仮定法と直説法
   現実の出来事＝「直説法」。想像上の出来事＝「仮定法」。
(1) 直説法：事実をありのままに述べる。
   It（＝The application form） *will* **look much better if you** *type* **it.**
   ※ if 節は「条件を表す副詞節」（現実にあり得ることを述べている。）
(2) 仮定法：事実に反することを仮定したり，実現しそうにないことを願望する。
   If I *were* a bird, I *would* fly to her.
   （もし私が鳥だったら，彼女のところに飛んで行くのに。）
   ※ if 節は，現実にはあり得ないことを仮定している点に注意。
2. 仮定法過去：現在の事実に反する仮定を表す。
   「もし（今）〜なら」〈If＋S＋過去形 ..., S'＋助動詞の過去形＋原形〜〉
   I *would* **(type it if I** *were* **you).** ※主節が前，if 節が後ろに来ている。
3. 仮定法過去完了：過去の事実に反する仮定を表す。
   「もし（あのとき）〜だったら」〈If＋S＋had＋過去分詞 ..., S'＋助動詞の過去形＋have＋過去分詞〜〉
   I *wouldn't have* **(recognized you), either, if someone** *had not mentioned* **your name.** ※主節が前，if 節が後ろに来ている。

EXERCISES

1　空所に入る最も適切な語句を，それぞれ下から選んで，番号で答えなさい。

(1) If you (　　　) enough money, why don't you buy a car?
   ① had　② have　③ have had　④ will have
(2) If I were a little younger, I (　　　) you in climbing the mountain.
   ① have joined　② join　③ will join　④ would join

(3) Jim (　　　). Even if he hadn't practiced, he still would have won.
　① didn't win the race　② lost badly
　③ should win　　　　　④ won the race easily

2　次の日本語を英訳しなさい。
(1) もし僕が君なら，彼を助けるだろう。
　_____, I would help him.
(2) もしジョン（John）がその試験に合格していたら，医者になっていただろうに。
　_____, he would have been a doctor.
(3) ジェーンはよくやったが，もっとうまくできただろう。
　Jane has done very well, but she _____.
(4) A : There is no milk in the refrigerator.
　　B : Oh, sorry. 昨日のうちに買っておけばよかったわ。
　_____ some yesterday.
(5) Tom : 急がないと飛行機に間に合わないぞ。
　　Ken : Don't rush me. There's plenty of time, Tom.
　_____.

3　次の指示に従って，英語で自由に書きなさい。
Suppose that you are going to a deserted island alone, where no one lives. You are allowed to bring one thing with you there. What would you like to bring and why? Write a sentence, using the following sentence pattern, and more, if possible.
"I would bring _____, because _____."

（例）I would bring a lighter, because fire is necessary for cooking, making me warm and protecting me from wild animals.

Can-do 8 　現実と想像上の出来事を区別して述べることができる

_____
_____

LISTENING & WRITING

1. Keiko is now back in Japan from the U.S. She is talking to Andrew over the phone, who used to be an exchange student from the Philippines.
   2人の対話の内容と合うように，下から適語を選び，必要ならば適切な形に変えて各文の空所に入れなさい。ただし，同じ語は2度使えません。

(1) If Andrew ア_____ in Japan a week longer, he イ_____ Keiko.

(2) Andrew said if his country ウ_____ a developed country like Japan, many of the street children エ_____ there.

(3) Andrew shows his love toward his country by saying, "Even if I オ_____ again, I カ_____ to be a Filipino."

| be, | bear, | find, | see, | stay, | want |

2. Keiko talks to Kate, the new exchange student from London.
   2人の対話の内容と合うように，(　　) 内から適切な語句を選びなさい。

(1) Keiko is very (pleased, annoyed) that Jane is going to come to Japan and stay with her family.

(2) Keiko has (often, seldom) talked about Jane to Kate.

(3) If Keiko (didn't stay, hadn't stayed) with Jane, she couldn't have had a good time in the U.S.

(4) It's easy for Kate to know how (excited, disappointed) Keiko is now.

PAIR & GROUP WORK

先生の指示に従い，ワークシートを使って進めなさい。

1. ワークシート（1）を使って，指示に従って空所を埋めなさい。

2. 空所を埋めた文のひとつを使って（6.（Bonus!）も含む），その人物になりきって，次の（例）のようにペアで自由に1分間会話を続けなさい。
（例）
Student A : If I had had breakfast, I wouldn't be hungry now.
Student B : Why didn't you have breakfast?
Student A : Because I got up late in the morning!
Student B : What did you do last night?
Student A : Well, I found a new game on my smartphone. It was too exciting!
Student B : That sounds great! What's that game? Tell me.
…

3. 空所を埋めた文のひとつを使って（6.（Bonus!）も含む），同じペアで次の（例）のようにその文を含んだ会話文（skit）を自由に創作してワークシート（2）に書きなさい。なお，選んだ文には必ず下線を引きなさい。語数としては80〜100語程度を目指しましょう。
（例）
Tom : Ken, you look very busy. What's happening?
Ken : Oh, Tom, I've got a lot of homework to do. Besides, I've got to finish all of it only a few days!
Tom : Oh, that's a pity. Is there anything I can do for you?
Ken : Thank you for saying so, Tom, but I'll do it myself. <u>If I didn't</u>

<u>have to do my homework, I could go to a movie tomorrow.</u>
Tom：Well, it can't be helped. Take it easy, Ken.

4. 4つのペアからなるグループを作り，それぞれのグループ内で上の3. で創作したskitをペアごとに発表し合います。その後，各グループの代表ペアが，クラス全体の前で発表します。

Can-do 9
人の言葉を別の人に伝えることができる

《関連文法事項：時制の一致と話法》

DIALOGUE

① A：How is John? I'm afraid he doesn't look very well these days.
　 B：Well, **he says every day that this climate does not suit his health and that he must go very soon**. But I don't think he must go.
② A：**The doctor said to me, "You had better go somewhere for a change of air."**
　 B：Sorry, but I can't hear you. What did you say?
　 A：Well, **the doctor advised me to go somewhere for a change of air**.

日本語訳

① A：ジョンの様子はどう？　最近元気がないみたいだけど。
　 B：どうもこの気候が身体に合わないのですぐにここを離れなければって毎日言っているよ。僕は，彼は離れる必要はないって思うけどね。
② A：「あなたはどこかへ転地療養に行ったほうがいい」って医者から言われたよ。
　 B：ごめん。ちょっと聞こえなかった。今何て言ったの？
　 A：医者がね，僕にどこか転地療養に行けって言うのさ。

表現のまとめ

　他人や自分の言葉を，引用符（" "）を用いてそのまま伝える方法を直接話法といい，一方，内容を自分の言葉に直して伝える方法を間接話法という。上記 DIALOGUE で言えば，①の太字部分は間接話法。②の最初のAのセリフは直接話法で，次のAのセリフは同じ内容を間接話法で言い換えている。

　基本的に，相手に客観的に物事を伝えたいという意識が強く働く場合には間接話法が使われ，一方，その場の雰囲気をより生き生きと伝えたいという意識が強く働く場合には，直接話法が使われる。

　同じ内容を表す場合でも，直接話法と間接話法では時・場所などを表す副詞や指示代名詞が異なる場合が多いが，機械的な転換ルールに縛られることなく，具体的な場面をイメージして述べることが重要である。

（例）1. Tom said, "I will leave here tomorrow."
　　　→Tom said (that) he would leave *there* (*the*) *next day* [*the following day*].

　　2. Yesterday Jane said, "I'll come here tomorrow morning."
　　　話し手が，もしJaneの言う「ここ（here）」に今いるならば，この文の間接話法は次のようになる。
　　　→Yesterday Jane said (that) she would come *here this morning*.

EXERCISES

1　空所に入る最も適切な語句を，それぞれ下から選んで，番号で答えなさい。

(1) His boss said to him, "Make up your mind by tomorrow."
　 = His boss told him to make up his mind (　　　).
　　① by the following day　② by a day later

③ till the last day   ④ till any day
(2) In 47 B.C., Julius Caesar said that (　　) won a great victory.
① does he   ② had he   ③ he does   ④ he had
(3) He said to me, "If you should fail in getting a job, what would you do?"
= He asked me what I (　　) do if I (　　) fail in getting a job.
① will / shall   ② will / should   ③ would / shall   ④ would / should

2 各文の（　　）内の語句を正しく並べ替えなさい。
(1) 「いっしょにテニスをしましょう」とヘンリーは私に言った。
Henry said to me, "Let's play tennis."
= Henry (me / should / suggested / that / to / we) play tennis.

(2) 「危険なことは何もしないでくださいね」と彼の奥さんは言った。
"Please don't do anything dangerous," said his wife.
= His wife (anything / asked / do / him / not / to) dangerous.

(3) 医師によれば，私は少し太り過ぎなので，もっと運動するようにとのことだった
The doctor said to me, "You are slightly overweight. You need to take more exercise."
= The doctor said I was slightly overweight (and / I / more exercise / needed / that / to take).

3 次の日本語を英訳しなさい。
(1) 彼は，「君ならこの質問に答えられるかもしれない」と彼女に言った。

He said to her, "_____ be able to answer this question."
= He _____ be able to answer that question.

(2) 叔母は私に気分があまり良くないのかと尋ねました。
My aunt said to me, "_____ feeling very well?"
= My aunt asked _____ not feeling very well.

4 次の指示に従って，英語で自由に書きなさい。
Write what someone said to you and you can never forget.
(例) My father said to me, "Change yourself, or you can't change others."

_____
_____
_____

LISTENING

1 Jane kept her promise with Keiko and has come to Japan! They are now at Kansai International Airport.
ジェーンと恵子の会話の内容と合うように，①②どちらか適切なものを選びなさい。

(1) Jane is happy to see Keiko again and Keiko
① is also happy to see Jane again.
② understands Jane's feeling.

(2) Keiko said to Jane,
① "When can we get together?"
② "Can we get together soon?"

(3) Then Jane said to Keiko,
① "I'll come to Japan to see you."
② "I would have come to Japan to see you."

2 On the first day of Jane's homestay with Keiko's family, she is now at the dinner table.

ジェーンと恵子の会話の内容と合うように，①②どちらか適切なものを選びなさい。

(1) Keiko's parents said to her,
   ① "Put our Japanese into English."
   ② "We put your Japanese into English."
(2) Keiko's father wanted to say,
   ① "I hope you'll enjoy this dinner."
   ② "Please help you by yourself."
(3) Keiko's mother said,
   ① "Jane doesn't look hungry. Please ask her if you have anything you don't like to eat."
   ② "Jane doesn't look hungry. Is there anything she doesn't like to eat?"

GROUP WORK

先生の指示に従い，ワークシートを使って進めなさい。

1. A，B，Cの3人のグループになり，机を合わせましょう。そして，配られるカードの束を，合わせた机の中央に，書いたものが見えない状態で表を伏せて置きます。指示があるまで，カードに触ってはいけません。

2. これから話法をポイントとした，伝言・指示ゲームを行います。グループ内で何回か同じことを繰り返しますが，各回について，最終的に誰かがあなたに何か質問をします。その質問に答えましょう。

3. 質問の伝わり具合についてお互いに評価します。相手からの質問はどれ

くらい適切にあなたに伝わったでしょうか。「評価シート」の「Ⅱ他の生徒に対する評価」に沿って，各自記入しなさい。

4. 最後にまとめのライティングの活動を行います。ワークシートを使って，この活動で印象に残っているやり取りを，以下の（例）にならって50〜80語程度の英語の文章にまとめて書きなさい。

（例）

I chose a card which says, "Do you have any favorite food?" I asked Yuta that question. I think everyone has their likes and dislikes about food. In fact, I like strawberry ice cream very much and said so to him. Surprisingly, Yuta answered, "My favorite food is ice cream." The same answer with me! However, his favorite is not strawberry but chocolate chips. Anyway, we promised to go to an ice cream shop in downtown someday in the near future.

Can-do 10
物事を順序だてて論理的に説明し，自分の考えや感情を表現することができる

《関連文法事項：接続詞，形容詞，副詞》

DIALOGUE　situation : a high school campus in the U.S.

Maki　: Guess what!
Sandy : What?
Maki　: This morning at the bus stop, I was greeted by two boys who were also there. I was **surprised** at first **because** at home in Japan strangers don't usually greet each other.
Sandy : Ours is a **pleasant** custom, isn't it?
Maki　: **Yes, I like it, but surprisingly, when** the bus came, they didn't let me go ahead. **Wasn't that impolite in your country?**
Sandy : **Not necessarily.** Some women think "ladies first" is an unfair custom.

日本語訳　場面：アメリカのある高校キャンパスで

マキ　　：ねえねえ，聞いて！
サンディ：うん？
マキ　　：今朝バス停で2人の男の子から挨拶されたのよ。最初びっくりしたわ。だって，日本ではふつう見知らぬ人同士では挨拶はしないもの。

Can-do 10　物事を順序だてて論理的に説明し，自分の考えや感情を表現することができる　63

サンディ：私たちの習慣っていいでしょ？
マキ　　：そうね，私は好きだわ。でも，バスが来て，私を先に乗らせてくれなかったのにはびっくりしたわ。それって，あなたの国ではちょっと失礼なことじゃないの？
サンディ：必ずしもそうとは言えないわね。「レディーファースト」は不公平な習慣だと考える女性もいるからね。

表現のまとめ

・本文中の because, but, when は，物事を順序だてて論理的に説明する際に用いられる接続詞の例である。接続詞以外でも therefore, thus, nevertheless, however, consequently, eventually などの副詞や，as a result [consequence], in consequence などの副詞句も，物事を順序だてて論理的に説明する際に有用である。
・本文中の surprised や pleasant といった形容詞，あるいは surprisingly といった副詞は話し手の感情や気持ちを表す形容詞や副詞の例である。
・Yes, I like it. や Wasn't that impolite?，そして，その問いに対する答えである Not necessarily. は話し手の考えを表現している。

EXERCISES

1　空所に入る最も適切な語句を，それぞれ下から選んで，番号で答えなさい。

(1) (　　　) she was tired, she decided to take the bus instead of walking home.
　① Although　② Ever since　③ No matter how　④ Since

(2) I am very (　　　) for what I said to her yesterday.
　① regret　② regretful　③ regrettable　④ regretted

(3) The temperature has been rising in recent years. (　　　) the sales of air conditioners are very high.

① As ② Because ③ However ④ Therefore

2 各文の（　　　）内の語句を正しく並べ替えなさい。
(1) 昨夜は雨が降ったに違いない。なぜなら，まだ草が濡れているからだ。
It must have rained last night, (for / is / still / the grass / wet).
_____

(2) これは農業と食物連鎖を脅かし，そしてその結果として，人の健康を脅かす。
This poses a threat to agriculture and the food chain, (and / consequently / health / human / to).
_____

3 次の日本語を英訳しなさい。
(1) 始発列車に乗るために，その日の朝は5時に起きた。
I got up at five that morning _____ the first train.
(2) 私はケンに起こったことを悲しく思う。
_____ about what happened to Ken.
(3) Tom：もっと一生懸命に勉強しろよ。さもないと試験に落ちてしまうぞ。
David：You, too, Tom.
Study harder, _____ fail in the exam.
(4) Tom：退屈な映画だったなあ。
Ken：Yes, indeed. I was half asleep from the middle of the movie.
_____.

4 会話が成立するように，5〜10語の文を書きなさい。
Tom：Why didn't Mary come to the party last Saturday?
Yoko：The reason was that _____
_____.

LISTENING & WRITING

1. Jane arrived in Japan and started to stay with Keiko's family. One day Jane arrived home and seemed to be angry somehow. Jane, Keiko and Hiroshi, who is Keiko's brother, are talking with one another.

(1) 以下の文章は3人の対話の内容を要約したものです。(　　)内には単語1語，下線部には2語以上が入ります。それぞれの空所を埋めて要約文を完成しなさい。

One day Jane got on a train, ア(　　) a Japanese boy spoke to her. He said he would like to talk to Jane in English. Jane didn't want to talk with the boy イ(　　) he talked to her just ウ ＿＿＿＿＿＿＿＿＿ his English. Hiroshi suggests to Jane that she should be more generous, エ(　　) she doesn't オ(　　) with him and tells him that she doesn't want to be treated like カ ＿＿＿＿＿＿＿＿＿.

(2) 次の質問に英語で答えなさい。

① Did Keiko understand what Jane said at first?
＿＿＿＿＿＿＿＿＿＿＿＿＿＿＿＿＿＿＿＿＿＿＿＿＿＿

② Where did the boy think Jane comes from?
＿＿＿＿＿＿＿＿＿＿＿＿＿＿＿＿＿＿＿＿＿＿＿＿＿＿

③ Does Jane think many Japanese people take it for granted that Jane is an American and can speak English?
＿＿＿＿＿＿＿＿＿＿＿＿＿＿＿＿＿＿＿＿＿＿＿＿＿＿

2. Jane and Keiko are walking along a street near a shrine. 会話の内容と合うように，各文の空所を埋めなさい。(　　)内には単語1語，下線部には2語以上が入ります。

1. Jane said, "It is ア (　　　) that today is a special day."

2. Jane got to know that the day was a special day イ (　　　　) almost all the children with their parents _____.

3. Jane didn't understand ウ (　　　) the children wore kimonos.

4. Jane found that a girl who was dressed エ (　　　) in kimono was coming toward her. She wanted to _____ of the girl.

PAIR WORK

先生の指示に従い，ワークシートを使って進めなさい。

1. ワークシート (1) を使って，指示に従って空所を埋めなさい。

2. ペアを組み，片方の生徒が1〜3の英文を，もう片方の生徒が4〜6の英文を，それぞれ担当します。教師の指示に従ってペアで会話を始め，合図とともに相手を変えながらペアでの会話を続けます。なお，1〜6以外で，自分のオリジナルの英文を作り，それを使って会話をしてもよいこととします（その「やり取り」のまとめが，以下の3.の（例）で紹介されています）。その際，最も印象に残っている会話をしたTop 3の相手の氏名を，終了後メモしておき，「評価シート」に沿って評価します。

（会話例）

Student A : I think my pet dog *Hana* is necessary in our daily lives, because she is so useful.

Student B : Useful? What do you mean by that?

Student A : Well, thanks to *Hana*, my grandfather takes a walk with her every day. It'll help him to keep healthy. And also,

Hana is a great comfort for all the members of my family. Do you keep any pets?
Student B : No, I don't. My mother doesn't like pets.
Student A : Oh, I see. Actually, at first, I wasn't interested in pets so much, either, but now *Hana* is part of my family. I cannot do without her.
…

3. まとめのライティングの活動を行います。ワークシート（2）を使って，上記2. で最も印象に残っている Top 1 の「やり取り」を以下の（例）のように 80 〜 100 語程度の英語の文章にまとめて書きなさい。

（例）

What I remember most is that Yuta said, "Smartphones are not necessary." I asked why. Then, he answered that they wasted our time. For example, they prevent us from concentrating on studying, because we receive the messages from our friends continually and endlessly, and we think we have to reply to them right away. Besides, smartphones can be a tool to bully other people or to be involved in some crimes. Smartphones are a source of a lot of troubles. That's what Yuta said to me, and now I quite agree with him.

評価シートとワークシート

Can-do 1 ★評価シート

I 自己評価

	evaluation	A	B	C	total score
構成	3つ以上の英文を書けたか	（できた：3点）	（おおむねできた：2点）	（あまりできなかった：1点）	／3
内容	because節を使うなどして英文をふくらませることができたか	（できた：3点）	（おおむねできた：2点）	（あまりできなかった：1点）	／3
内容	印象的な英文を紹介できたか	（できた：3点）	（おおむねできた：2点）	（あまりできなかった：1点）	／3
	グループ内での話し合いを活発に行えたか	（できた：3点）	（おおむねできた：2点）	（あまりできなかった：1点）	／3
態度	ジェスチャーやアイコンタクト，笑顔といった態度はとれたか	（できた：3点）	（おおむねできた：2点）	（あまりできなかった：1点）	／3 ／15

II グループ発表の評価・感想【理解や同意の程度を3（高）～1（低）で評価する】

発表グループ	評点（観点1）	評点（観点2）	観点3	観点4
グループA	3　2　1	3　2　1		

グループB	3　2　1	3　2　1		
グループC	3　2　1	3　2　1		
グループD	3　2　1	3　2　1		
グループE	3　2　1	3　2　1		
グループF	3　2　1	3　2　1		
グループG	3　2　1	3　2　1		
グループH	3　2　1	3　2　1		
グループI	3　2　1	3　2　1		
グループJ	3　2　1	3　2　1		

Can-do 2 ★ワークシート【Sheet A】

1.
   1. I have been to _____ before.

   2. I have seen _____ before.

   3. I have read _____ before.

   4. I have heard / listened to _____ before.

2. 上の1.の４つの英文を書いた人は … **Name**：_____
   （特定できた後に，サインしてもらう．）
   〜インタビューメモ〜

3. インタビューの結果のまとめ（written by No.（　）Name: _____）

_____

_____

_____

_____

★評価シート【Sheet B】

I 自己評価

	evaluation	A	B	C	total score
構成	インタビューの結果を50〜70語程度の英語でまとめることができたか	(できた: 3点)	(おおむねできた: 2点)	(あまりできなかった: 1点)	／3
内容	4つの英文を適切に書くことができたか	(できた: 3点)	(おおむねできた: 2点)	(あまりできなかった: 1点)	／3
内容	4つの英文を書いた人物の特定を，英語でやり取りしながらスムーズに行えたか	(できた: 3点)	(おおむねできた: 2点)	(あまりできなかった: 1点)	／3
内容	インタビューとして自然なやりとりを行い，メモすることができたか	(できた: 3点)	(おおむねできた: 2点)	(あまりできなかった: 1点)	／3
内容	メモをもとに，聞き取った内容を整理して口頭で発表することができたか	(できた: 3点)	(おおむねできた: 2点)	(あまりできなかった: 1点)	／3
態度	ジェスチャーやアイコンタクト，笑顔といった態度はとれたか	(できた: 3点)	(おおむねできた: 2点)	(あまりできなかった: 1点)	／3 ／18

II 他の生徒に対する評価【3：すばらしい　2：まぁまぁ　1：もっと練習を】

発表者の氏名	評点（観点1）	評点（観点2）	評点（観点3）	評点（観点4）	合計
①　(　　　　　)	3　2　1	3　2　1	3　2　1	3　2　1	/12
②　(　　　　　)	3　2　1	3　2　1	3　2　1	3　2　1	/12
③　(　　　　　)	3　2　1	3　2　1	3　2　1	3　2　1	/12
④　(　　　　　)	3　2　1	3　2　1	3　2　1	3　2　1	/12

	コメント（良かった点・改善点など）
①	
②	
③	
④	

Can-do 3　★ワークシート【Sheet A】

Pair： Class（ 　 ）　　No.（ 　 ）　Name:＿＿＿＿＿＿＿＿＿＿＿
　　　　　　　　　　　　No.（ 　 ）　Name:＿＿＿＿＿＿＿＿＿＿＿

1. Questions：
（例）Do I always have to pay with cash in shopping in Japan?
(1) ＿＿＿＿＿＿＿＿＿＿＿＿＿＿＿＿＿＿＿＿＿＿＿＿＿＿＿＿＿＿＿

(2) ＿＿＿＿＿＿＿＿＿＿＿＿＿＿＿＿＿＿＿＿＿＿＿＿＿＿＿＿＿＿＿

(3) ＿＿＿＿＿＿＿＿＿＿＿＿＿＿＿＿＿＿＿＿＿＿＿＿＿＿＿＿＿＿＿

2. Advice： ＊Advisers：No.（ 　 ）　Name:＿＿＿＿＿＿＿＿＿＿
　　　　　　　　　　　　　No.（ 　 ）　Name:＿＿＿＿＿＿＿＿＿＿
（例）It depends. I think you should ask a clerk before paying.
To (1) ＿＿＿＿＿＿＿＿＿＿＿＿＿＿＿＿＿＿＿＿＿＿＿＿＿＿＿＿＿

To (2) ＿＿＿＿＿＿＿＿＿＿＿＿＿＿＿＿＿＿＿＿＿＿＿＿＿＿＿＿＿

To (3) ＿＿＿＿＿＿＿＿＿＿＿＿＿＿＿＿＿＿＿＿＿＿＿＿＿＿＿＿＿

3. Dialogue：（例）本冊の"Example"参照。
A（an American）:＿＿＿＿＿＿＿＿＿＿＿＿＿＿＿＿＿＿＿＿＿＿＿

　　　　　　　　　＿＿＿＿＿＿＿＿＿＿＿＿＿＿＿＿＿＿＿＿＿＿＿

　　　　B（you）:＿＿＿＿＿＿＿＿＿＿＿＿＿＿＿＿＿＿＿＿＿＿＿

　　　　　　　　　＿＿＿＿＿＿＿＿＿＿＿＿＿＿＿＿＿＿＿＿＿＿＿

A（an American）:＿＿＿＿＿＿＿＿＿＿＿＿＿＿＿＿＿＿＿＿＿＿＿

　　　　　　　　　＿＿＿＿＿＿＿＿＿＿＿＿＿＿＿＿＿＿＿＿＿＿＿

★評価シート【Sheet B】

I 自己評価

	evaluation	A	B	C	total score
構成	内容のある Dialogue を書けたか	(できた：3点)	(おおむねできた：2点)	(あまりできなかった：1点)	／3
内容	初めて日本を訪れるアメリカ人になったつもりで質問はできたか	(できた：3点)	(おおむねできた：2点)	(あまりできなかった：1点)	／3
	説得力のあるアドバイスはできたか	(できた：3点)	(おおむねできた：2点)	(あまりできなかった：1点)	／3
	会話として自然なやりとりであったか	(できた：3点)	(おおむねできた：2点)	(あまりできなかった：1点)	／3
態度	ジェスチャーやアイコンタクト，笑顔といった態度はとれたか	(できた：3点)	(おおむねできた：2点)	(あまりできなかった：1点)	／3 ／15

II 他の生徒に対する評価【3：すばらしい　2：まぁまぁ　1：もっと練習を】

発表ペアの氏名	評点（観点1）	評点（観点2）	評点（観点3）	評点（観点4）	合計
① (　　)，(　　)	3　2　1	3　2　1	3　2　1	3　2　1	／12
② (　　)，(　　)	3　2　1	3　2　1	3　2　1	3　2　1	／12
③ (　　)，(　　)	3　2　1	3　2　1	3　2　1	3　2　1	／12
④ (　　)，(　　)	3　2　1	3　2　1	3　2　1	3　2　1	／12

	コメント（良かった点・改善点など）
①	
②	
③	
④	

Can-do 4 ★ワークシート（1）

Class (　) No. (　) Name: _____
・Partner： No. (　) Name: _____

Mary：happy

[her teacher / praise]
*praise 〜：〜を褒める

Jack：angry

John：troubled

[his teacher / tell / clean the classroom alone]

Keiko：disappointed

創作 skit　取り上げた人物：(　　　　　) *名前を記入する

_____
_____
_____
_____
_____
_____

評価シートとワークシート　75

★ワークシート (2)

Class (　)　No. (　)　Name: _____
・Partner: 　No. (　)　Name: _____

Mary : happy

_____
_____

Jack : angry

[his classmates / tease]
*tease〜：〜をからかう

John : troubled

_____
_____

Keiko : disappointed

[her boyfriend / drop]
*drop〜：〜(付き合っている相手)をふる

創作 skit　取り上げた人物：(　　　　　　　　)＊名前を記入する

_____
_____
_____
_____
_____
_____
_____

★評価シート

Ⅰ　自己評価

	evaluation	A	B	C	total score
構成	50〜80語程度の創作skitを書けたか	(できた：3点)	(おおむねできた：2点)	(あまりできなかった：1点)	／3
内容	それぞれの人物に何が起きたのかをペアの相手に正しく伝えることができたか	(できた：3点)	(おおむねできた：2点)	(あまりできなかった：1点)	／3
内容	それぞれの人物に何が起きたのかを聞き取り，正しく書くことができたか	(できた：3点)	(おおむねできた：2点)	(あまりできなかった：1点)	／3
内容	創作skitをスムーズに演じられたか	(できた：3点)	(おおむねできた：2点)	(あまりできなかった：1点)	／3
態度	ジェスチャーやアイコンタクト，笑顔といった態度はとれたか	(できた：3点)	(おおむねできた：2点)	(あまりできなかった：1点)	／3 ／15

Ⅱ　他の生徒に対する評価【3：すばらしい　2：まぁまぁ　1：もっと練習を】

発表ペアの氏名	評点(観点1)	評点(観点2)	評点(観点3)	評点(観点4)	合計
①(　)，(　)	3　2　1	3　2　1	3　2　1	3　2　1	／12
②(　)，(　)	3　2　1	3　2　1	3　2　1	3　2　1	／12
③(　)，(　)	3　2　1	3　2　1	3　2　1	3　2　1	／12

	コメント（良かった点・改善点など）
①	
②	
③	

評価シートとワークシート　77

Can-do 5　★ワークシート【Sheet A】

```
        Class (  )   No. (  )   Name: _____
            Partner :  No. (  )   Name: _____
```

1. Task 4 (Listening & Writing)

_____

_____

_____

_____

_____

_____

_____

_____

【MAP】
＊Use another sheet of paper or a copy of a map.

2. Task (2) (Pair & Group Work) : The space for taking notes.

★評価シート【Sheet B】

I 自己評価

	evaluation	A	B	C	total score
構成	リスト及びその理由を書けたか	(できた：3点)	(おおむねできた：2点)	(あまりできなかった：1点)	／3
内容	パートナーに好みの場所を説明できたか	(できた：3点)	(おおむねできた：2点)	(あまりできなかった：1点)	／3
内容	パートナーの話を聞いて，自分の好みと好みではない場所を伝えられたか	(できた：3点)	(おおむねできた：2点	(あまりできた：1点)	／3
内容	会話として自然なやりとりであったか	(できた：3点)	(おおむねできた：2点)	(あまりできなかった：1点)	／3
態度	ジェスチャーやアイコンタクト，笑顔といった態度はとれたか	(できた：3点)	(おおむねできた：2点)	(あまりできなかった：1点)	／3 ／15

II 他の生徒に対する評価【3：すばらしい 2：まぁまぁ 1：もっと練習を】

発表ペアの氏名	評点（観点1）	評点（観点2）	評点（観点3）	評点（観点4）	合計
① (　　)，(　　)	3 2 1	3 2 1	3 2 1	3 2 1	/12
② (　　)，(　　)	3 2 1	3 2 1	3 2 1	3 2 1	/12
③ (　　)，(　　)	3 2 1	3 2 1	3 2 1	3 2 1	/12
④ (　　)，(　　)	3 2 1	3 2 1	3 2 1	3 2 1	/12

	コメント（良かった点・改善点など）
①	
②	
③	
④	

Can-do 6 ★ワークシート

Class（　）　No.（　）　Name：_____
・Partner：　No.（　）　Name：_____

1.「第1回雑学クイズ王コンテスト」得点：（　　）点 ※満点：（　　）点

2. ペアで作成した英文：
   _____
   _____
   _____

3.「第2回雑学クイズ王コンテスト」得点：（　　）点 ※満点：（　　）点

4. I was most interested in （　　　　）'s statement. He / She （Circle the either one） said, _____
   _____
   _____
   _____
   _____
   _____
   _____
   _____
   _____
   _____

★評価シート

I 自己評価

	evaluation	A	B	C	total score
構成	100語程度の「振り返り英作文」を書けたか	(できた：3点)	(おおむねできた：2点)	(あまりできなかった：1点)	／3
内容	「雑学クイズ王コンテスト」では英文の内容を正しく聞き取れたか	(できた：3点)	(おおむねできた：2点)	(あまりできなかった：1点)	／3
内容	「比較」の表現を用いて，ペアで適切な英文を作ることができたか	(できた：3点)	(おおむねできた：2点)	(あまりできなかった：1点)	／3
内容	ペアで作った英文を正しく全体に伝えられたか	(できた：3点)	(おおむねできた：2点)	(あまりできなかった：1点)	／3
態度	ジェスチャーやアイコンタクト，笑顔といった態度はとれたか	(できた：3点)	(おおむねできた：2点)	(あまりできなかった：1点)	／3 ／15

II 他の生徒に対する評価【3：すばらしい　2：まぁまぁ　1：もっと練習を】

Top 3の発表ペアの氏名	評点（観点1）	評点（観点2）	評点（観点3）	評点（観点4）	合計
① (　　)，(　　)	3　2　1	3　2　1	3　2　1	3　2　1	/12
② (　　)，(　　)	3　2　1	3　2　1	3　2　1	3　2　1	/12
③ (　　)，(　　)	3　2　1	3　2　1	3　2　1	3　2　1	/12

	コメント（良かった点・改善点など）
①	
②	
③	

Can-do 7　★ワークシート（1）

Class（　　）　列番号：（　　　　）

★ **Passage A**

You must study English hard,

or _____.

Besides, _____.

But _____.

In other words, _____.

Thus, _____.

because _____.

★ **Passage B**

We are not dependent on smartphones too much,

because _____

_____.

To put it more simply, _____.

However, _____.

Moreover, _____.

Therefore, _____.

though _____.

★ワークシート（2）

Class ( )　No. ( )　Name: _____

★ **Passage A**

You must study English hard,

or _____.

Besides, _____.

But _____.

In other words, _____.

Thus, _____.

because _____.

★ **Passage B**

I don't like to wear the school uniform,

because _____

_____.

To put it more simply, _____.

However, _____.

Moreover, _____.

Therefore, _____.

though _____.

★評価シート
I 自己評価

	evaluation	A	B	C	total score
構成	ワークシート (2) をすべて書くことができたか	(できた：3点)	(おおむねできた：2点)	(あまりできなかった：1点)	／3
内容	接続詞やつなぎの副詞等を理解して、ワークシート (1) で自分の担当箇所を書くことができたか	(できた：3点)	(おおむねできた：2点)	(あまりできなかった：1点)	／3
内容	ワークシート (1) で仲間の書いた英文を理解し、また、自分の書いた英文を正しく仲間に伝えられたか	(できた：3点)	(おおむねできた：2点)	(あまりできなかった：1点)	／3
内容	自分たちの列の書いた文章を、他の生徒に正しく伝えられたか	(できた：3点)	(おおむねできた：2点)	(あまりできなかった：1点)	／3
態度	適切な音量で発表し、ジェスチャーやアイコンタクト、笑顔といった態度はとれたか	(できた：3点)	(おおむねできた：2点)	(あまりできなかった：1点)	／3 ／15

II 他の生徒に対する評価【3：すばらしい　2：まぁまぁ　1：もっと練習を】

発表列の番号	評点(観点1)	評点(観点2)	評点(観点3)	評点(観点4)	合計
① 列番号（　　）	3　2　1	3　2　1	3　2　1	3　2　1	/12
② 列番号（　　）	3　2　1	3　2　1	3　2　1	3　2　1	/12
③ 列番号（　　）	3　2　1	3　2　1	3　2　1	3　2　1	/12
④ 列番号（　　）	3　2　1	3　2　1	3　2　1	3　2　1	/12
⑤ 列番号（　　）	3　2　1	3　2　1	3　2　1	3　2　1	/12
⑥ 列番号（　　）	3　2　1	3　2　1	3　2　1	3　2　1	/12
⑦ 列番号（　　）	3　2　1	3　2　1	3　2　1	3　2　1	/12

	コメント（良かった点・改善点など）　Can-do 7
①	
②	
③	
④	
⑤	
⑥	
⑦	

Can-do 8 ★ワークシート (1)

Class ( ), No. ( ), Name: _____

例にならって，自分が次のそれぞれの状況にいると仮定して下線部を埋め，文を完成しなさい。

(例) You don't understand Ms. White because she doesn't speak very clearly.
You say: If Mr. White <u>spoke clearly</u>, I <u>would understand her</u>.

1. You can't go to a movie tomorrow because you have to do your homework.
   You say: If I _____,
   　　　　 I _____.

2. You were able to buy the brand-new bicycle because you worked part-time.
   You say: If I _____,
   　　　　 I wouldn't _____.

3. You're hungry now because you didn't have breakfast.
   You say: If I _____,
   　　　　 I _____.

4. You live in Tokyo and you don't like it.
   You say: I wish I _____.

5. You didn't study math a lot, and you've failed your math test.
   You say: I wish I _____.

6. 《Bonus! Give it a try!》
   You _____.
   You say: _____
   _____

★ワークシート（2）

Class （　）　No. （　）　Name: _____
　　　　　　　　　The Partner's Name: _____

★創作 skit：

_____
_____
_____
_____
_____
_____
_____
_____
_____
_____
_____
_____
_____

【メモ】

★評価シート
I　自己評価

	evaluation	A	B	C	total score
構成	80～100語程度の創作skitを書けたか	（できた：3点）	（おおむねできた：2点）	（あまりできなかった：1点）	／3
内容	仮定法と直説法を理解して，ワークシート（1）の下線部を埋め，英文を完成することができたか	（できた：3点）	（おおむねできた：2点）	（あまりできなかった：1点）	／3
内容	ワークシート（1）で書いた英文を使って，ペアで1分間会話を続けることができたか	（できた：3点）	（おおむねできた：2点）	（あまりできなかった：1点）	／3
内容	創作skitをスムーズに演じられたか	（できた：3点）	（おおむねできた：2点）	（あまりできなかった：1点）	／3
態度	適切な音量で発表し，ジェスチャーやアイコンタクト，笑顔といった態度はとれたか	（できた：3点）	（おおむねできた：2点）	（あまりできなかった：1点）	／3　／15

II　他の生徒に対する評価【3：すばらしい　2：まぁまぁ　1：もっと練習を】

発表ペアの氏名	評点（観点1）	評点（観点2）	評点（観点3）	評点（観点4）	合計
①（　　），（　　）	3　2　1	3　2　1	3　2　1	3　2　1	／12
②（　　），（　　）	3　2　1	3　2　1	3　2　1	3　2　1	／12
③（　　），（　　）	3　2　1	3　2　1	3　2　1	3　2　1	／12

	コメント（良かった点・改善点など）
①	
②	
③	

Can-do 9 　★ワークシート

Class (　　)　No. (　　)　Name: _____

My most unforgettable interaction:

_____
_____
_____
_____
_____
_____
_____
_____
_____
_____
_____
_____
_____
_____

【メモ】

★評価シート

I 自己評価

	evaluation	A	B	C	total score
構成	50〜80語程度の「やり取り」のまとめを書けたか	(できた：3点)	(おおむねできた：2点)	(あまりできなかった：1点)	／3
内容	間接話法を使って正しく伝えられたか	(できた：3点)	(おおむねできた：2点)	(あまりできなかった：1点)	／3
内容	直接話法を使って正しく伝えられたか	(できた：3点)	(おおむねできた：2点)	(あまりできなかった：1点)	／3
	指示を正しく聞き取ることができたか	(できた：3点)	(おおむねできた：2点)	(あまりできなかった：1点)	／3
態度	適切な音量で伝え，ジェスチャーやアイコンタクト，笑顔といった態度はとれたか	(できた：3点)	(おおむねできた：2点)	(あまりできなかった：1点)	／3　／15

II 他の生徒に対する評価【3：すばらしい　2：まぁまぁ　1：もっと練習を】

グループ内の他の生徒の氏名	評点（観点1）	評点（観点2）	評点（観点3）	評点（観点4）	合計
①	3　2　1	3　2　1	3　2　1	3　2　1	／12
②	3　2　1	3　2　1	3　2　1	3　2　1	／12
③	3　2　1	3　2　1	3　2　1	3　2　1	／12

	コメント（良かった点・改善点など）
①	
②	
③	

Can-do 10　★ワークシート（1）

Class（　　）, No.（　　）, Name: _____

次の（　　　）内に適当な接続詞やつなぎの副詞（句）を入れなさい。
また，下線部は各自で自由に埋めなさい。

1. I like _____, and （　　　）, I believe in _____.

2. My favorite subject is _____; （　　　）, I like to study it.

3. I think _____ is / are necessary in our daily lives, （　　　） it / they is / are so useful.

4. I must _____.
   （　　　） I'll regret my high school life.

5. I want to tell a lie that _____
   next April the 1st, （　　　） April Fools' Day.

6. I don't like _____,
   （　　　） I'll try to like it.

【メモ】

★ワークシート (2)

Class (　)　　No. (　)　　Name: _____

My most unforgettable interaction:

_____
_____
_____
_____
_____
_____
_____
_____
_____
_____
_____
_____
_____
_____
_____
_____
_____

【メモ】

★評価シート

I 自己評価

	evaluation	A	B	C	total score
構成	80〜100語程度の「やり取り」のまとめを書けたか	(できた：3点)	(おおむねできた：2点)	(あまりできなかった：1点)	／3
内容	接続詞や副詞などを理解して，ワークシート (1) の下線部を埋め，英文を完成することができたか	(できた：3点)	(おおむねできた：2点)	(あまりできなかった：1点)	／3
内容	ワークシート (1) で書いた英文を使って，ペアで即興の「やり取り」ができたか	(できた：3点)	(おおむねできた：2点)	(あまりできなかった：1点)	／3
内容	ペアの相手を変える方式をスムーズに行えたか	(できた：3点)	(おおむねできた：2点)	(あまりできなかった：1点)	／3
態度	適切な音量で発表し，ジェスチャーやアイコンタクト，笑顔といった態度はとれたか	(できた：3点)	(おおむねできた：2点)	(あまりできなかった：1点)	／3 ／15

II 他の生徒に対する評価【3：すばらしい 2：まぁまぁ 1：もっと練習を】

Top 3の相手の氏名	評点（観点1）	評点（観点2）	評点（観点3）	評点（観点4）	合計
①	3 2 1	3 2 1	3 2 1	3 2 1	/12
②	3 2 1	3 2 1	3 2 1	3 2 1	/12
③	3 2 1	3 2 1	3 2 1	3 2 1	/12

	コメント（良かった点・改善点など）
①	
②	
③	

■ 著者紹介

萩野　俊哉　（はぎの　しゅんや）

　　　1960 年新潟県小出町生まれ，柏崎市育ち。
　　　1984 年東北大学文学部英語学科卒業。
　　　中越学園中越高等学校　校長

【主な著書】

『ライティングのための英文法』（大修館書店）［「外国語教育研究奨励賞」（語研）受賞］，『コミュニケーションのための英文法』（大修館書店），『英文法指導 Q&A — こんなふうに教えてみよう』（大修館書店），『言語活動がアクティブ・ラーナーを育てる — 生徒の英語であふれる授業』（大修館書店），『英語授業プリント改善講座』（大修館書店），文部科学省検定教科書 *Genius English Course. I-II Rev.*, *Genius English Readings. Rev.*（以上大修館書店，共著）など。

Can-do English
— 英語コミュニケーション能力を高めるために —

2025 年 3 月 1 日　初版発行

■ 著　　者 ──── 萩野俊哉
■ 発 行 者 ──── 佐藤　守
■ 発 行 所 ──── 株式会社　大学教育出版
　　　　　　　〒700-0953　岡山市南区西市 855-4
　　　　　　　電話（086）244-1268　FAX（086）246-0294

© Shunya Hagino 2025
ISBN978-4-86692-290-4